MONEY WHIZ KIDS

MONEY WHIZ KIDS

DOCTOR WISE

Publishing-World

CONTENTS

CHAPTER 1

What Is Money?

Once upon a time, in a colorful town named Sunnyville, there lived a group of curious kids who loved to play and learn new things. One sunny day, they started wondering about something very interesting: **What is money?**

"Money is what you use to buy things," said Mia, holding up a shiny coin.

"But where does it come from?" asked Alex, looking at a paper bill with a picture on it.

"Let's find out!" exclaimed Omar, always ready for an adventure.

Together, the friends set out on a journey to discover everything they could about money. They first visited Mr. Green, the owner of the local candy store.

"Money is like magic tokens," Mr. Green explained with a smile. "You give me money, and in return, I give you candy. It's our way of trading."

"Wow, so money is for buying things!" said Mia.

Next, they visited the Sunnyville Bank. Mr. Patel, the bank manager, showed them different types of money from around the world.

"See, children, money can be coins, like these, or paper, like these bills. Different places have different money, but they all do the same thing – help us exchange goods and services."

The kids saw money with different colors, shapes, and sizes. They were amazed!

"So money is not just about buying things; it's also about trading things fairly," Alex realized.

"That's right," Mr. Patel nodded. "Money also helps us save for something big in the future."

Thinking about the future made them all excited. They imagined saving money for bikes, toys, and even a trip to the zoo!

As the sun set over Sunnyville, the kids returned home, their minds buzzing with new ideas about money.

"I'm going to start saving my allowance," declared Omar.

"And I'll use my money wisely," added Mia.

As they drifted off to sleep that night, they all dreamed of becoming Money Whiz Kids, ready to explore more money mysteries in the days to come.

You can color this picture. Have fun!

CHAPTER 2

How Do I Get Money?

Afher learning what money is, the Money Whiz Kids were full of new questions. The next day, they gathered under the big oak tree in Sunnyville Park, wondering, "How do we get money?"

Mia remembered something her mom said, "Money is earned by working. When you do a job, you get paid with money."

"That's it!" exclaimed Omar. "We can earn money by doing jobs!"

"But what kind of jobs can we do?" Alex wondered, looking a bit puzzled.

The friends put on their thinking caps and came up with some bright ideas:

1. Lemonade Stand: "We can set up a lemonade stand!" said Mia. "We'll make fresh lemonade and sell it to people in the park. It's a perfect job for sunny days!"
2. Pet Sitting: Omar had another idea. "Lots of neighbors have pets. We can offer to take care of them when they are busy. Pet sitting can be fun, and we'll earn money too!"

3. Yard Work: Alex thought about helping in gardens. "We can help people with yard work. Like raking leaves, watering plants, or even weeding. Everyone appreciates a tidy garden!"

4. Car Wash: "What about washing cars?" suggested Mia. "We can set up a car wash station. It'll be fun, and people always like a shiny, clean car!"

5. Crafts and Art Sale: Omar, who loved arts and crafts, had a creative idea. "We can make things like bracelets, paintings, or clay pots and sell them. People love handmade stuff!"

6. Helping with Chores: "We can also help our families with extra chores," added Alex. "Maybe our parents will give us a small amount of money for helping out more than usual."

The kids were excited about these ideas. They decided to try them out one by one.

"Remember," Mia said, "earning money means being responsible and doing our best!"

They all agreed. The Money Whiz Kids were ready to start their new adventure in earning money, learning about hard work, responsibility, and the value of money.

As the day ended, they felt proud and excited about their plans. They were not just learning about money; they were learning to be smart, hard-working, and creative – just like true Money Whiz Kids.

Coloring Book

CHAPTER 3

What Should I Do With My Money?

After the Money Whiz Kids started earning money, they faced a new question: "What should we do with our money?" They gathered in Mia's backyard, under the apple tree, to brainstorm ideas.

"Let's spend it all on toys!" Alex said excitedly, thinking about the new video game he had seen.

"But what if we need money later for something important?" Mia pondered, always the thoughtful one.

Omar had an idea. "Let's learn how to handle our money wisely!" he suggested.

Together, they came up with some smart ways to handle their money:

1. **Saving for the Future**: "We should save some of our money for later," Mia proposed. "We can keep it in piggy banks or even open a savings account at the bank."

2. **Spending Wisely**: "It's okay to buy things we like, but we need to think before we spend," Omar advised. "We should ask ourselves if we really need it or just want it."

3. **Budgeting**: "We can make a budget," Alex suggested. "It's like a plan for how to use our money. We can decide how much to save, spend, and maybe even give away."

4. **Donating to Charity**: Mia thought about helping others. "We can give some money to charity or people who need help. It's a good way to be kind and helpful."

5. **Investing in Learning**: "We can also use money to learn new things," Omar added. "Like buying books or taking classes in things we're interested in."

6. **Setting Goals**: "Let's set goals for what we want to save for," said Alex. "Like a new bike, a family trip, or a college fund."

The children realized that handling money was not just about spending but making smart choices for their present and future.

They decided to make jars with labels: Save, Spend, and Share. Every time they earned money, they would think carefully and divide it among the jars.

As they placed their first coins into the jars, they felt proud. They were not just earning money; they were learning to be responsible and thoughtful with it.

The Money Whiz Kids were on their way to becoming smart money managers, learning valuable lessons that would help them for the rest of their lives.

CHAPTER 4

Money Whiz Kid Budget

The Money Whiz Kids had learned a lot about earning and handling money. Now, they were curious about making a budget. "What's a budget, and how do we make one?" Alex asked as they sat in the Sunnyville Library.

Mia, who had read a book about it, explained, "A budget is a plan for your money. It helps you decide how to spend and save your money wisely."

"Let's make our own Money Whiz Kid Budget!" Omar suggested enthusiastically.

Here's how they created a simple budget:

1. **List Your Money**: "First, we need to know how much money we have," said Mia. They listed all the money they earned from their lemonade stand, pet sitting, and other jobs.
2. **Set Your Goals**: Omar thought about what they wanted to save for. "We need goals, like saving for a new bike, a school trip, or a gift for someone."
3. **Divide into Categories**: "Let's divide our money into different parts," Alex proposed. They made categories like 'Savings',

'Spending', and 'Sharing'. Each category got a part of their total money.

4. **Decide How Much to Save**: Mia suggested, "We should save at least a little bit of all the money we get." They decided a portion of their money would go straight into their 'Savings' jar.

5. **Plan Your Spending**: "We can use the 'Spending' part for things we want to buy," said Omar. They agreed to spend only a certain amount and to think carefully before buying anything.

6. **Remember to Share**: "Don't forget about helping others," Mia reminded them. They set aside some money for charity or gifts.

7. **Keep Track**: "We should write down what we do with our money," Alex said. They made a simple chart to keep track of their earnings and how they used their money.

8. **Adjust as Needed**: "Our budget can change," Omar noted. "If we earn more or our goals change, we can adjust our budget."

The kids felt proud as they finished their first budget. It was a simple plan, but it made them feel like real Money Whiz Kids. They learned that a budget helps you make smart choices with your money.

Now, whenever they earned money, they used their Money Whiz Kid Budget to help them decide how to use it. They were learning to be smart and responsible, not just with money, but in life.

CHAPTER 5

Ways To Save

With their Money Whiz Kid Budget in place, the next adventure for Mia, Alex, and Omar was to explore different ways to save money. They gathered in their favorite spot in the park, ready to share their ideas.

"Saving money is like a game," said Mia. "The more we save, the closer we get to our goals!"

Here are the ways they found to save money:

1. **Piggy Banks**: "We can start with piggy banks," suggested Omar. "It's a fun way to see our savings grow. Every coin we put in gets us closer to what we're saving for!"
2. **Savings Jars**: Alex had a different idea. "What about jars for different goals? One for a toy, one for a trip, and one for a big wish like a new bike. We can decorate them and watch our savings split into different dreams!"
3. **Savings Account**: "We can open a savings account at the bank," said Mia. "It's like a piggy bank, but the bank keeps it safe for us. And we can watch our money grow with interest!"

4. **Cutting Costs**: Omar thought about spending less. "If we spend less on things we don't really need, we can save more. Like choosing a smaller toy or making our own snacks instead of buying them."

5. **Earning More**: "Doing more small jobs can help us save more," Alex pointed out. "Like an extra hour of pet sitting or helping neighbors."

6. **Gift Money**: Mia remembered her birthday. "Sometimes, we get money as gifts. We can save some of it instead of spending it all."

7. **Saving Challenges**: "Let's make saving a challenge!" Omar proposed. "Like a 'no-spend week' where we only use things we already have, or a 'save-the-change' game where we save all the small coins we get."

The Money Whiz Kids were excited to try these saving methods. They understood that saving money wasn't just about putting it away, but about making smart choices and finding creative ways to grow their savings.

As they tried different ways to save, they learned valuable lessons about patience, discipline, and the joy of reaching their goals.

"Saving money can be fun and rewarding," they all agreed. They were proud to be Money Whiz Kids, not just learning about money, but growing into smart savers and wise spenders.

CHAPTER 6

The Saving Challenge

The Money Whiz Kids had learned many ways to save money. Now, they were ready for a new challenge. Mia came up with an idea during their Saturday morning meetup at the community center.

"Let's have a **Saving Challenge!** It will teach us about delayed gratification."

"What's delayed gratification?" asked Alex, curious about the new term.

"It means waiting for something better in the future instead of wanting something right now," explained Mia.

So, they decided to set a goal: Save enough money for a group trip to the Sunnyville Amusement Park in three months. Here's how they tackled the Saving Challenge:

1. **Setting the Goal**: "First, we need a clear goal," said Mia. They calculated how much money they would need for the trip and set that as their target.

2. **Understanding Delayed Gratification**: Omar shared, "Delayed gratification is like waiting to eat a marshmallow now so we can have two later. It's about being patient for a bigger reward."

3. **Resisting Temptation**: Alex admitted, "It's hard not to buy cool stuff now, but if we wait, we can have even more fun on our trip." They learned to resist immediate temptations to reach their bigger goal.

4. **Tracking Progress**: Mia suggested, "Let's make a chart to track our savings. We can see how close we are to our goal." This helped them stay motivated and focused.

5. **Finding Extra Ways to Save**: They looked for more ways to save, like making gifts instead of buying or doing extra chores for some additional allowance.

6. **Encouraging Each Other**: "We need to encourage each other," said Omar. They shared saving tips and cheered each other on during weekly meetings.

7. **Celebrating Small Wins**: Every time they reached a small goal, they celebrated. Mia said, "It's important to recognize our efforts, even the small ones."

8. **Learning Patience**: The challenge taught them patience. Alex realized, "Waiting isn't so bad when we have a fun goal at the end!"

Finally, the day of the trip arrived. The Money Whiz Kids had reached their goal! They felt a huge sense of accomplishment.

At the amusement park, as they laughed and played, they knew the wait was worth it. They had not only saved enough for the trip but had also learned an important life lesson: good things come to those who wait and work for them.

ABOUT THE AUTHOR

Travis jokingly refers to himself as a psycho biologist or a psycho farmer, because of his seemingly radical (by many people's perspectives) approach to gardening and the use of trees and bushes for landscaping.

He was born and raised, and is still a resident of, along with his awesome wife, in southeast Wisconsin.

He is a father of two children – 1 daughter, 1 son.

A science geek since early childhood, he majored in Biology at the University of Wisconsin.

He also attended Oregon State University where he studied Permaculture Design.

Later, he attended Keller Graduate School of Management, where he received a Master of Business Administration (MBA) degree.

He has a passion for writing, constantly learning, gardening and growing things, life itself, and questioning conventional wisdom.